A Day in the Life
30 prompts to inspire and develop a regular writing habit

By

Darren R Hill

A Day in the Life

30 prompts to inspire and develop a regular writing habit

Copyright © 2015 by Darren R Hill
All rights reserved. This book or any portion thereof may not be reproduced or used in any manner whatsoever without the express written permission of the publisher except for the use of brief quotations in a book review.

Published by waoao
www.waoaomediasolutions.com

Cover artwork copyright Suzi Blu all rights reserved
www.suzibluart.com

ISBN-13: 978-1507818459
ISBN-10: 1507818459

Darren R Hill has worked in the publishing business for around twenty years. He has experience across the whole spectrum of publishing from editorial to management, commissioning to writing. He has coached writers from idea to publication. He has one novel published, one non-fiction book published and has written hundreds, if not thousands, of published articles, blog posts, newsletters and post-its.

A lot of this book was written and edited with the following soundtracks playing in the background for which the author is eternally grateful:
The Antlers' *Hospice*, This Temple Eden's *Music to Make Art By* and the whole St Vincent catalogue.

"For someone who dreamt of writing but didn't know where to start"

Let's begin...

I want to be a writer. How can I be a writer? It's a question many ask. It's a question many answer, by offering techniques, structures and lessons in grammar. However, despite all this help, the answer to the question is really quite simple.

"How do I begin?"

That, my friend and fellow wordsmith, is often the hardest part. It throws up questions. When can I write? How do I write? What do I write? The when and how can only be answered by yourself, but here are a few ideas. Set the alarm a little earlier and spend just 15 minutes each morning writing, then add another 15 minutes to your day and jot a few words before you go to sleep. Go to a coffee shop or park for lunch and take a notepad or journal with you and write. If you travel by train, use that time to write. Or make a choice to not watch a particular program on TV and replace the time you would have spent watching with writing time. If we want to commit to writing it is amazing how much time we can find. And, always carry a notebook with you, for those moments of inspiration or when you find yourself with a little time on your hands.

How you write is up to you. I would suggest starting to write longhand, with a pen / pencil and book. It is easier to use a digital device, and once you get in the swing of things then by all means use one, however there is something magical about crafting the letters, words and sentences yourself – you'll feel more connected to the words. I think writing in journals and notebooks has a permanence that digital does not. If, like me, you're worried about using a nice journal and making a mess, writing rubbish and constantly crossing out, then two things. Firstly, don't. Putting lines through what you write will help you develop your craft. Secondly, if you really, really can't bear using that nice journal, then buy some cheap exercise type books, you can get them for ridiculously low prices. Actually three things, there is space in this book too!

"What do I write?"

That leaves us with the biggest question of all, what do I write? Many websites offer writing, or other art, prompts. They are great for finding a little guided inspiration. However, the majority of these prompts and ideas are not connected. At the end of the week, month or year, you'll have plenty of words, but they won't be part of a unified piece.

A Day in the Life, has two main goals.

1 To help you write regularly for 30 days

2 To write a piece of prose that grows each day and on completion fits together like a fitty-together thing (technically we call this a plot, but let's not get bogged down in author speak just yet.)

Writing isn't just about random words, those words need to connect, make sense or form some sort of cohesion (even if the cohesion is hard for anyone other than the writer to understand). The words need to be collected together to make a whole, this might be a poem, a short story, a novel or a work of non-fiction. In other words, apologies for the pun, they need to be complete, or finished.

As you'll find out, once you have defined what complete means, you can break that definition or rule. I want to encourage you to break as many rules as you can, that's where, in my humble opinion, creativity comes from. You can ~~copy~~ be inspired by others, but to make a creative step you need to do something different, however subtle that might be. This book provides you with the basis for writing something that will hold together and be complete. At the same time I will encourage you throughout to step outside the lines, find your own voice and create your own unique work.

A Day in the Life contains 30 prompts. Each prompt will inspire you to write about one moment of a character's day. I'll give you a phrase to get you going, but you don't need to use that. There is space to write notes or even your draft. Whatever you do, the main goal is to write.

"To be a writer, you merely need to write."

The back story; the building block

All stories have characters. Characters are one of the essential building blocks in writing fiction. The more you know about your character the more you can write about them and the more your reader will find them believable.

A Day in the Life will help you explore a character in depth. From taking your character from daybreak to day's end, you'll understand how they deal and react to many things.

Every character that ever graced the words of a story had a daily routine. We may not get to know what that routine is, the ebb and flow of the narrative obscure and supersede it, but it is there. One well-known story writing process begins with a daily routine, something that occurs every day in a character's life, or group of characters' lives. This routine continues until 'one day ...', the routine is disrupted and an adventure begins.

A Day in the Life is all about the routine. Your routine, or the routine of your character. You'll write what happens to them from the moment they wake until the moment they sleep, and then some. Through this process you'll draw on memories and observations, two of the most important tools in your writing toolbox.

But before you begin...

A Day in the Life provides detailed prompts for each day, however there is plenty of wiggle room for you to be creative within these. One wiggle is to choose your character. There are no restrictions to who, or in fact, what, your character is. You can use yourself, and describe the events in a first person style, 'I woke this morning to the sound of dogs greeting the milkman.' You can use someone else and describe events in the third person, 'They woke to the sound of the dogs welcoming the post.' You could be a little surreal, 'I woke to the sound of the dogs playing monopoly.' You could write a fantasy story, 'They woke to the sound of the dogs discussing the storming of the castle.' In space? 'I woke to the sound of a dog barking; the Excelsior's AI had developed an animal fixation.' The options are almost limitless. The beauty of A Day in the Life is that you can choose again and again what character and what setting you want to use.

Choose your character, your setting and your perspective. At the back of the book is a character note sheet to help. This sheet is photocopiable and there will also be a downloadable version from www.yourimaginality.com/a-day-in-the-life

The final piece of the puzzle, before we begin, is you, the would-be writer. That's the point, would-be. Are you ready to take the step and be that writer? I said before you only have to write. Only is a little four letter word, but like another four letter word, it is very powerful. Only has a companion word, if. If you write every day you'll be a writer. If you write every day for 30 days you will develop a writing habit. If you write about 300 words each day for 30 days you'll have 9000 words. 9000 words is a great length for a short story. But *only if*.

If you write you'll be a writer, that's the **only** thing you need to do.

Do you want to be a writer?

It's time to commit.

A form to sign with all my commitments

```
I will write for 30 days

My character:

My setting:

My perspective: First / Third* Person

Beginning on

Ending on

I will use the following time to write:

Signed:
Date:
```

* Delete as applicable. First person is 'I woke up to a delightful, dazzling day.' Third person is 'Gwendoline Bothersome-Smythe woke up to a dreary, damp day.'

01 The moment you wake

The first prompt is all about the moment you wake, those very first moments as your day begins. Does the alarm rouse you? Do you drift into consciousness? Are you followed by the memories of a dream? What are your first thoughts or your final dream moments? What is the first thing seen or heard - or not seen and heard?

With these thoughts in mind you can begin the writing process. You take memories and moments and begin to craft them into your own prose. You bring those thoughts into the world you are creating on the page in front of you. First or third person, past, present or future, it's all your choice.

Keep focussed on that one moment, this isn't about the rest of the day, just that one moment. You'll find that one moment can extend a long way. However, this isn't about the amount of words you can write. This is about beginning the writing process, and forming a writing habit. We have set aside some time to write and now we begin to draw on our memories and imagination.

"My eyelids flicker. ..."

NOTES

Draw on your memories, the emotions, the sensations that you have and write. There is no minimum or maximum word count, just write and see where your creativity leads you.

Mirror, mirror 02

You are awake and have made it to prompt number two, and the bathroom. Yes, I said number two and bathroom in the same sentence.

This prompt is all about looking in the mirror and writing down what you see, or don't see. As you gaze into the mirror, what is there? Is the mirror misted from a hot shower you've just had, or is the mirror the first thing you see as you open your eyes after a bleary walk? Are you met by an old or young face, or a face you don't recognise?

You could let your imagination run here, what if you were a vampire, or an alien, or have you lost your memory, how would you describe the reflection? Or you could keep things a lot more personal, describing every nook, cranny, ridge and depression etched on your face. When you get to my age that takes a little longer. Mirror, mirror on the wall, what is that reflection, it's your call!

If you are writing a day in a science fiction setting, what differences are there in the bathroom of the future, or on a space ship? What if you, or your character is not in a house? If you are travelling or sleeping rough, where and how do you wash?

"My face isn't reflecting the radiance of the sun. ..."

NOTES

Draw on your memories, the emotions, the sensations that you have and write. There is no minimum or maximum word count, just write and see where your creativity leads you.

03 Breakfast at the author's

Awake and washed and dressed (perhaps), you manage to make your way to the kitchen. It's breakfast time. You've not been invited to Tiffany's, or even to the local diner, or truck stop. This is the moment you make it to your kitchen in the morning.

What do you do? Rush to get the coffee going? Fumble for some bread to put in the toaster? Prepare a lavish feast for yourself? What sounds do you hear, the urban sprawl assaulting your peace or the birdsong and wild sounds of the countryside? Is it dark or light, has morning truly arrived or are you stuck in the pre-dawn gloom?

Is breakfast a moment of peace and solitude or a battleground as the multitude fuel themselves for the day ahead... but don't think too far ahead. Write and describe these moments, from arriving in the kitchen to finishing your food and drink, or perhaps you don't have time to eat, that's valid too.

What about those fantasy and science fiction pieces you may be writing? Do you have a kitchen? If not where do you eat? How do you eat? What do you need to prepare and do in order to break your fast?

One thing to remember, a semi-rule, although please feel free to break it, is to stick to the prompt itself and not wander off. These prompts are time specific, so try not to step into the next prompt. This isn't really a problem, so it isn't really a rule. It's just like, a recommendation. It's a bit like feeling the shape of the present and guessing what it is before you unwrap it, you still get the present but the surprise isn't quite the same.

"It had often been said that breakfast was the most important meal of the day. ..."

NOTES

Draw on your memories, the emotions, the sensations that you have and write. There is no minimum or maximum word count, just write and see where your creativity leads you.

04
Open sesame

You're now ready to face the world, it is time to step outside, to open your front door. This prompt is all about capturing one moment and drawing as much from it as you can. Once again don't stray too far beyond this prompt. This isn't a time to think about the day ahead, but the moment when you come face to face with it.

Write about the moment you open your front door. Was it an easy thing to do, did you have to fight your way through to make a path, or is your house minimal and decluttered? Are you actually in a house? - These prompts are only guidelines, so feel free to use them as jumping off points. As you open the door what do you see, what sounds greet you, what smells? Do you feel other things? Is it hot, cold, wet, dry? How would you describe the sky? Is anybody walking by?

This is just one moment, the moment you open your door and look out. However, there is so much that you can find in just one, seemingly mundane, moment. It is a skill that all artists have, and as a writer, a skill you can develop. Take just one moment and write about it. Describe it in such detail that the reader is there, with you. Use simile, metaphor, poetic, or just plain descriptive language to expand the moment and bring it to life.

Your imagination can really run wild if you're not writing about a day on planet earth. What differences are there elsewhere in the universe, or in space? How does the air taste, is it recycled? How does a different sun colour things?

"My eyes shut by reflex as the sun's brightness greeted me. ..."

NOTES

Draw on your memories, the emotions, the sensations that you have and write. There is no minimum or maximum word count, just write and see where your creativity leads you.

The journey is the destination
05

You could be going anywhere, the destination is up to you. You've left your house, flat or wherever, and you're now on your journey. What form of transport are you taking? Private or public transport offer completely different feelings and levels of control. Likewise, where you are going makes a difference to how you feel and how concerned you are with the time. The need to get to work, or school, is more time-sensitive than a trip to the shops or another clandestine meeting, or is it?

The other thing to think about is whether you are on your own or with others. Will there be conversations, or will you retreat into yourself and be more reflective? Do you need to meet someone *en route*, or have a chance meeting?

Your setting and genre will have an obvious influence on what you write. A journey in space or some fantastical land will be a little different to a city commute. Closeness, or being able to relate to the characters you write about, is core to engaging your readers. Closeness to your readers own situation becomes difficult in strange new worlds, however this is where sharing emotions and feelings are important. Whatever the place and whatever the tools, the emotions are the same, they will bring closeness for your readers.

We learn as much from the journey as the destination. How often have you achieved something and then thought, is that it? This is because the journey was the real achievement. This prompt allows you to explore this. However, this isn't about arriving, that's another prompt, this is just the journey.

"The sound echoed as my foot scraped across the pavement ..." **NOTES**

Draw on your memories, the emotions, the sensations that you have and write. There is no minimum or maximum word count, just write and see where your creativity leads you.

Arrive and shine
06

The journey is complete. You are in the process of arriving, and this is today's prompt. I find it a quirk of English that arrive is such a finite verb. It relates to a specific moment, but that moment can contain so much. To be honest, we arrive at every moment, we are constantly arriving. To arrive is no more finite than to breathe, or hope, or love.

Back to today's prompt. After the journey, you reach your destination. It is time to explore this new place and describe the new environment. After a journey, we should be someplace else. Comparing two, or more places, is a wonderful way to describe your new location. What are the differences between here and where you were? Are you now in the dry and warm after a wet and cold journey? Is this new location antiseptic and minimal compared to your loved and comfortable home?

How do you feel about these differences? What emotions does this new place bring to the surface? Again try not to dive into the day ahead, we are only arriving, and not yet doing. For those on a more fantastical journey through their day, does this new place bring memories or notions of hope, or dire warning, or more unanswered questions?

We arrive at every moment, but a specific arrival after a specific journey is what we are trying to capture today. If you are arriving at a place you haven't been to before, your senses will be bombarded with new information. If your destination is the same everyday, then those sensations will be couched in multiple memories. The destination is up to you, but it is time to write about your arrival.

> "The entrance loomed before me, greeted by Max Headroom instead of a fanfare or murder hole ..."

NOTES

Draw on your memories, the emotions, the sensations that you have and write. There is no minimum or maximum word count, just write and see where your creativity leads you.

The daily plan it 07

This is all about thinking and planning. Planning what your 'character' is doing. It is time for them to think about what needs to be done, what is their plan for the day? This doesn't mean doing those things, just thinking the day through.

Wherever your character has arrived, it is time to think about the day ahead. This could be at work, at school, at the shops, or a space station, an alternative earth. How do they plan what needs to be done? Do they use a diary, a journal, or phone? Do they keep scraps of paper in their purse or bag, which they need to hunt and track down? Are they waiting for some divine intervention? Are the stars in the firmament, at their right conjunction? Do the cards reveal a path that needs to be taken? Or, is their day planned for them? Is the day ahead just another list handed to them? Can they access their preferred method for planning? What if their phone is dead?

What about feelings? Do they feel free or controlled? Are they happy with the path that lies ahead or do they wish that they could walk another? It is time to explore both the process and the emotions involved in how they plan, or don't plan their days.

Feel free to explore this in whatever way you want. This could be very close to home, your own day, or the day of someone you know – remember though, that bit in books about all the characters supposedly being fictitious ;) . It could be your fantasy character, do they follow a course set for them, are they using traditional methods to plan their day, or do you need to create some new form of guide? Are they helped by some super artificial intelligence, or some not so super AI?

"Once again I had forgotten to fill in my diary properly ..." **NOTES**

Draw on your memories, the emotions, the sensations that you have and write. There is no minimum or maximum word count, just write and see where your creativity leads you.

08 Ring, ring

The phone rings. This is such a regular occurrence that we don't think about it. However, there is so much that can be said, thought about, or in this case, written on the subject, that it makes an ideal creative writing prompt.

First there is your location, where are you and what are you doing when the call comes in? Are you busy at work, bored at work, rushing round the shops, sitting bored at home, or on some secret mission? Are you in a public or private space, will your conversation be overheard? Does that matter?

What device is the call coming in on? Is it a mobile, your work phone, or perhaps you're walking by a call box? Does the phone have caller ID? Is the call from someone you know or is the caller's identity withheld?

How do you feel as the phone rings, or vibrates? Is this a call you want to have or would rather it happen at some other time, or never? Do you have any idea what the message will be when you answer the phone, how are you feeling just before you accept the call?

Finally, and not forgetting, there is the call itself, the conversation. Is the call urgent or mundane? Does the message stop you in your tracks or merely confirm something you already know? What does the voice on the other end of the line sound like, what emotions does their voice convey? Is the voice human? If you are using a mobile, will your battery hold out?

Phones ring all the time. Let's explore that event in today's writing prompt and get creative with the call and our feelings. If you are exploring a fantasy or sci fi narrative, then use the questions above but invent your own communication method. How does the message get to you in this setting? Remember it is the emotions and feelings that make the connection with your readers.

"It was a gentle, soothing, rhythmic feeling, but that was the last moment of calm ..."

NOTES

Draw on your memories, the emotions, the sensations that you have and write. There is no minimum or maximum word count, just write and see where your creativity leads you.

Time for tea   09

The morning has been busy so far, or has it? That's the thing about living in an imaginary world that you are creating. It may have been busy, quiet or somewhere in between. You may have slayed dragons or barely managed to have your first thoughts. It's your creative world, your writing prompts.

Despite what you may, or may not to have got up to so far, it is now time for a break. What better opportunity for a break than to have a cup of tea, my preferred option, or a coffee. It is something most of us do each day. We stop, we catch a breath, and have a drink.

So where are you having your drink? Are you at work, taking a moment from the daily grind, on your own or with others; a communal cup? You may be out and about and decide to pop into the coffee shop? Again, this could be on your own or with friends you are meeting. Perhaps you meet someone while you are in the shop. Or, you may just sit there, on your own reflecting on what might have been.

This is an exercise in stopping and thinking. Write what is inside your mind, your thoughts and ideas, the emotions that you bring with you to these quiet moments. I actually find it a great place to write, the coffee shop, the background noise and the characters there are always a source of inspiration.

Your setting will shape what you write. How you take a break in an office will be very different to on a space ship or space station, or mediaeval castle or a cross world quest. Let your setting shape what you write, be true to your character's surroundings.

"An exhale, closed eyes and relaxing of my shoulders signalled that it was time for a break ..."

NOTES

Draw on your memories, the emotions, the sensations that you have and write. There is no minimum or maximum word count, just write and see where your creativity leads you.

10 Back to work, back to reality

Tea time is over it is now time to get back to work, and in our case writing. Today's writing prompt is about work, sorry, but it forms such a substantial part of our lives, I can't let it pass. However, you may find this more interesting and challenging than you think. Remember these prompts call upon your memories, but also your imagination, this doesn't have to be you that you're writing about.

You are in the office, the place you work. Your desk is in front of you. What is on it? How do these items help you do your job? What is your job? What does your daily routine consist of while seated at this desk? Or are you in an office? Is your job at an art studio, music studio or some other creative place? Again how do the items in your studio help, or perhaps hinder, your creative work?

Do you work from home or at home? The same questions apply, what are you doing, how do you do it and what helps or hinders? You can also explore your feelings as you do your work. Are you happy doing it or would you rather be some place else? Do you imagine you are elsewhere as you work, transforming your work into an imaginary journey?

If you are working a fantasy idea, you can still use the thoughts and questions above. Just because your character is in deep space, or in another realm, doesn't mean they don't have work to do. We all work in one way or another, whether employed, self-employed or unemployed. We all work, that is reality.

One thought just occurred as I was writing this. Perhaps your character is unable to work for some physical or mental condition. You could explore the memories they have of working and the frustrations they now face. As always, these are your prompts, explore and enjoy.

"The pile of paper shouted loud, demanding my attention ..."

NOTES

Draw on your memories, the emotions, the sensations that you have and write. There is no minimum or maximum word count, just write and see where your creativity leads you.

Let's do lunch 11

Lunchtime is a moment in the day that many of us relish. So what better moment of the day to choose for our writing prompt. It is lunchtime, the morning is done with, the rest of the day stretches before you, but before you head into the afternoon, it is time for lunch.

There are so many options for you to write about here. Do you have your lunch at work, in the office, at your desk? Why? What do you eat? Have you brought food with you or do you need to find something to buy locally? Are you disturbed by others as you try to take a break?

Or, do you go out for lunch, a local restaurant or cafe, or bistro? Do you go alone or with friends? If friends, who are they, why do you all go together? Are you meeting someone special for lunch? Are you having a secret rendezvous? There are plenty of options for you to let your creativity shine here... or even your own private fantasies!

Talking of fantasy, if you are using these prompts for your own fantasy writing, then don't forget things like lunch and eating. It is the everyday things, done in the extraordinary fantasy settings, that add depth to your writing. How do you get your lunch if you are in space, or journeying across a desert? Is it pre-packed and pre-cooked, or do you need to find it from the world you are wandering through?

Lunch is a time to enjoy, to celebrate being alive, a time to feed our bodies. It is also a wonderful opportunity to stretch our writing muscles and be creative with this moment that is so fundamental to our being. Enjoy the prompt and let your imagination fly.

"Sometimes it was the most difficult decision to make, the menu staring back at me offered no help ..."

NOTES

Draw on your memories, the emotions, the sensations that you have and write. There is no minimum or maximum word count, just write and see where your creativity leads you.

12 It's siesta time

There is a part of me that is drawn to the Mediterranean lifestyle. It might be the sun, the food or the party atmosphere, but if I'm honest it is something a little less active – I am drawn to the idea of siesta. With this very much in my mind, if not yours, it makes it to today's writing prompt.

You've had lunch, either rushed or relaxed, and now you hit the early afternoon, lull. A real siesta may not be an option, depending on where you are, or where your character is. However, this is what we'll look at. We'll be focussing on feelings, both physical and mental.

You're body is full, content. It has been fed and now wants to rest. Are you able to let your body relax? There is always plenty on our mind, so how do you put this aside for a moment of rest? Are you back at your work desk, or have you taken a walk to the park or somewhere else? How does your body feel, sluggish, tired?

You may be able to take a real break, a real siesta. Are you at home or on holiday? Where do you go to take your break? Do you need to find a space for yourself away from the others?

As you relax how does your body feel and how does your mind feel? What relaxes first, your body or your mind? Do you need to calm your thoughts before your body does likewise or the other way round? Do you need to go through a meditative routine to calm your thoughts?

If you are exploring theses prompts through a fantasy narrative, what additional things do you need to take note of? Do you need to find a safe place in order to rest? Are there things you need to set in motion to allow you to take a break, such as automatic pilot or similar - vital if you are in a spaceship. When you write, the more detail you can add, the more believable your narrative becomes. This is something to hold on to when writing fantasy.

Enjoy your siesta... but write first.

"I rubbed my eyes, but it did little to rouse me ..."

NOTES

Draw on your memories, the emotions, the sensations that you have and write. There is no minimum or maximum word count, just write and see where your creativity leads you.

13 Something, but what?

Let's stretch those creative juices with today's writing prompt, not that you haven't already. It is time to see how far we can come up with an idea that's a little more abstract. I don't mean surreal, although with all these prompts feel free to interpret them as you wish, what I mean is an idea that springs from you, from your subconscious, from the creative idea centre that you feed and nourish... It is there!

You're back at work, back into your routine for the day. Likewise, you may be back at home, or out shopping, it is your day after all. If you have your fantasy hat on, then your day may be a little more out of the ordinary, but you still find yourself back in the routine of scientific experiments, data collection or dragon quest. This is where I want you to stretch those creative muscles.

Detail the regular, the mundane, the *what is going on* of your afternoon. Be descriptive and draw the reader into your world. Now, hint that something is wrong. Something isn't quite right, but you don't know what it is. This is where you can really push yourself to develop your writing. This is all about describing and detailing your emotions. You need to explore these feelings without saying what is actually wrong. You are distracted, but you can't quite put your finger on it.

Emotions and feelings enable a writer to connect with their reader. The more you can express the feelings of your characters, the more real they become. It isn't easy, and you may struggle at first but have a go, and above all, have fun. What is getting your character all worked up and distracted, distracted enough to disrupt their day?

"It wasn't a sound or something I could see, but it was tangible none the less ..."

NOTES

Draw on your memories, the emotions, the sensations that you have and write. There is no minimum or maximum word count, just write and see where your creativity leads you.

14 Shocking the system

You're back to the daily routine. You might be at work, at home or on your fantasy journey, but everything is on track and progressing nicely. That's where today's writing prompt begins. You need to explain that everything is fine and hunky dory and going well. You are getting on with what needs to be done and looking forward to a worry-free afternoon... until.

Something happens that changes things. Your carefully planned day, or afternoon, is shattered by something. This can be anything from a phone call from the boss asking for an emergency piece of work or information, to a major family incident, to whatever. Wherever you are this information changes things and disrupts your day.

What we want to explore is the change from one state of calmness and serenity to panic and disruption. How does this impact on your character? What changes happen to you emotionally and physically? What words do you use to explore these changes? One idea that can be quite helpful is to use a thesaurus. This will help extend your vocabulary and remind you of words that might be on the tip of your tongue.

Enjoy the change in emotional states during this prompt. It might be a challenge, but then writing everyday is. Have fun though, going from utter calm to complete panic. Not all journeys measure great distances in miles!

"There was a calmness that didn't anticipate the moments to follow ..." **NOTES**

Draw on your memories, the emotions, the sensations that you have and write. There is no minimum or maximum word count, just write and see where your creativity leads you.

Comfortably calm 15

The working hour is done. The rest of the day, and all the possibilities that evening and night bring, lies ahead. First, though, it is time to celebrate the completion of work. You have got through the stresses and strains of both normal and surprise work. You can relax.

How do you relax? If you are at the office do you have time to talk with colleagues, or even catch a quick drink with them at the local coffee shop, wine bar or pub? Do you write the email to the boss asking for that promotion seeing how you managed to handle today's pressure? At home do you call a friend, message on Facebook or pour yourself a GnT?

You are on a roll, what about sending that text, email or phone call to someone that you like, or care about? You may want to share your good fortune with others, make a donation to charity? Sit and talk to the person begging out on the high street?

The choice, as always, is yours. Explore how you feel and what you do when the task at hand is done. How do you celebrate, not for the major victories, but the small ones? You may want to explore that despite all you have achieved today, you are still not good enough to have a reward?

The fun of the evening still lies ahead, but pause and realise that you have already achieved so much. If you are on a fantasy writing journey, then the same questions are relevant, but again how does your specific situation impact the words you write? This is also the 15th writing prompt, you're halfway through. That is something to feel good about!

"I interlocked my fingers, stretched out my arms; the clicks and cracks as my fingers bent back on themselves echoed ..."

Draw on your memories, the emotions, the sensations that you have and write. There is no minimum or maximum word count, just write and see where your creativity leads you.

School run

16

Your work day is over, but you aren't the only one who has finished. The school day is finished as well. This is the focus of our prompt today, the school run, picking up the children.

Either you are off to the school to pick up the children, or you see children leaving school on your journey home. If you are using these prompts in a fantasy setting, then you can explore your own memories of childhood and how you felt having finished your learning for the day. The same applies in a science fiction narrative, although if you are in a large enough environment, you may well have a school in space.

What are your feelings as you head to pick the children up? Do you look forward to seeing them again? What are your hopes for their future, as they leave the school building? If you are not picking up your own children, what are your hopes and fears for them as they grow up into the world? Do you wish that one day you were picking up your own kids? Is there a memory that needs sharing to explain why you are not picking children up, has your character lost children?

How we relate and respond to the next generation, either our own, or in general, is a good source of inspiration for our writing. You could explore questions they have, or discuss something they have learnt that day. Have they learnt something you didn't know, or are you able to add to their knowledge? If you are not picking up your own children, you can explore how much you learnt at school. Did you enjoy your time there, or were you glad to get out?

Using our own memories in writing is a valuable tool. Childhood memories often shape how we feel today. Sometimes writing about these events can be therapeutic as we review our memories and feelings.

> "The smile was as broad and bright as the afternoon sun, the child as bubbly as when they had disappeared behind the school gate ..."

NOTES

Draw on your memories, the emotions, the sensations that you have and write. There is no minimum or maximum word count, just write and see where your creativity leads you.

What's that song?

17

Like all forms of art, music touches our lives in ways other things can't. Music can speak to our soul and dance with our feelings. Today's prompt is nice and simple and allows us to explore our emotions and memories, through the inspiration of music.

Wherever you are and whatever you are doing, you hear a song, a piece of music. This could be on the radio, your portable music player, or, if in a fantasy setting, a wandering minstrel, or similar. The song is random though. It isn't one that you intended to play, or hear, so it comes as a surprise, or shock, when it is heard.

What is the song? What memories does it bring back? Are those memories linked to the first time you heard the song? Or do the lyrics of the song remind you of an event, a person, a moment from your past? Are your feelings positive or negative? Does the song remind you of happier or sadder times? Does hearing the song remind you of unfinished business or inspire you to start something new?

One skill that many writers use, especially, it seems, in fantasy settings, is to write their own songs, or poems, and bring them into their writing. Is this something you want to attempt from today's prompt? Have fun, and let the music take you on an adventure today.

"Like an echo from a disused tunnel the sound revived memories long abandoned ..."

NOTES

Draw on your memories, the emotions, the sensations that you have and write. There is no minimum or maximum word count, just write and see where your creativity leads you.

18 Daydream believer

Do you daydream? Do you find yourself drifting off and thinking of something unrelated to what you're doing? Today's prompt is all about exploring those moments and using your imagination.

Set the scene by describing what you are doing. This can be anything, but my personal preference is to be drinking a cup of tea... I like tea, I may have mentioned that before! Once the scene is set, it is time to let your thoughts drift, and begin to daydream.

What comes to mind? Where do your thoughts head? Do you dream of that ideal relationship, that romance that you wish would happen? Do you think of what might have been, or what could be, if you made different decisions? Do you imagine yourself as a secret agent or some other world changing role?

If you are using these prompts in a fantasy setting, does your daydream present itself as a vision? Do you see something that you need to note, or act on? Is it a vision of impending doom or possible hope? Do you have a more lucid dream of events to come?

It's possible that daydreaming is potentially dangerous. You could be operating some machinery, or driving, or charting unknown star systems as you hurtle through space.

When it comes to daydreaming, you can write about anything. Let your imagination flow and your creative writing flourish.

> "One moment I was focussed, the next I was elsewhere, as if I had jumped through time and space ..."

NOTES

Draw on your memories, the emotions, the sensations that you have and write. There is no minimum or maximum word count, just write and see where your creativity leads you.

19 A night out

The evening is ahead of you. You are going out. This can be to anywhere you want, perhaps an evening meal, or a rendezvous with someone special, or not so special? The choice is yours, however, first you have to get ready.

This prompt is about the practicalities of getting ready to go out for the night. What do you need to remember? What do you need to do? What are the things, or rituals, you go through before you go out? Do you shower, bath, rest, relax? Do you spend time fretting over what you will wear? How do you decide the appropriate clothes for the evening?

How do you feel about the night ahead? Are there things you would like to do before the evening is over? Are there things you don't want to happen? Use your memory to write your words, drawing on the things you do and the emotions you have had in the past. Then put them into your creative writing.

For those creating a fantasy series, the same questions apply, but placed into the world you have created. Does your world include hot showers, hair straighteners and designer clothes? In a space fantasy, are there new inventions that make getting ready easier, or more of a burden? If you are alone and not able to go out, you could be planning and getting ready for some form of communication. On a spaceship or space station how do you maintain relationships with those you love and care about?

> "A look in the mirror is followed by a deep breath, this was going to take a little bit of work ..."

NOTES

Draw on your memories, the emotions, the sensations that you have and write. There is no minimum or maximum word count, just write and see where your creativity leads you.

The dinner party

20

It's time to eat, it's dinner time. However, food isn't the focus of this writing prompt. We're going to explore the art of conversation, it's time we had a talk. The dinner party is a great setting for conversation. In fact, it is a great idea for the creation of plays, stories and life itself.

The art of conversation is very much alive in today's prompt. The dinner party setting is totally up to you. You could be having an intimate meal and chat with a partner, or friend. You could be having a fantasy discussion with your favourite characters or heroes from history. You could be on your spaceship and eating whilst you talk with the ship's sentient computer.

Set the scene and then launch into the conversation. Speech in stories isn't straight forward. It makes you think about accents, idioms and personalities. The back story of characters drives the things they say and how they act. Are they timid, aggressive, quiet, loud? All these traits are thought through, yet they may never be explicitly mentioned in the conversation. This makes you think a lot more about your characters.

The topic of conversation is up to you, but try to make the majority of what you write speech. (I'm currently writing a short story that is just a conversation between two people.) A conversation is a great way to explore science fiction or fantasy writing. As mentioned above you could be talking to a computer, but what about aliens, or mythical creatures? Do you need an interpreter?

Enjoy your meal and enjoy the conversation. Write the words that are normally spoken, and see where the conversation leads. Let your characters say things that you, the writer, wouldn't normally say yourself. For once you are in charge of the conversation. Let the words flow.

" 'So, when did you discover that you had such a passion for this,' he asked ... "

Draw on your memories, the emotions, the sensations that you have and write. There is no minimum or maximum word count, just write and see where your creativity leads you.

21 Play away

It's time to play. Time to chill out and spend time playing a game with a child, or group of children. The idea behind this prompt is to think like a child. Get inside the head of young person as they play and put those thoughts on to paper, or screen.

Choose a game to play, perhaps a favourite from your own childhood. Draw on those memories as you write. What is the difference between how you remember the game and how you play it now, as an adult? Do you find it more, or less enjoyable?

Think of the child you are playing the game with? Do they stick to the rules? Do they question the rules? What is the most important part of the game for them? Do they make fun of you as you try to play? Does the game have 'strict' rules or is it creative? *LEGO* can be both: would you follow the instructions or build from imagination?

How easy do you find it to immerse yourself in the imaginative world of the child or children? Does the game bring out forgotten memories, times of innocence and happiness? Or memories of sadness?

If you are writing in a fantasy style, do you need to create a game? Can you describe the game without writing all the rules, or do you need to completely define a game? If you are stuck in space how do you play the game with a child? You could remember when you played a game or you could attempt to play it over video conference, or has 3D holographic video conferencing been invented?

Go forth and play, there should always be time for a little play here and there.

> "I looked at the assortment of moulded plastic strewn across the floor, this would be an adventure ..."

NOTES

Draw on your memories, the emotions, the sensations that you have and write. There is no minimum or maximum word count, just write and see where your creativity leads you.

Just one kiss 22

Today's prompt is all about the intimate. It is time for your character, to have a physical moment with another. It is time for a kiss!

The setting is, as always, pretty much yours to choose. It could be at the end of an evening out, or a chance meeting. It could be following a heated argument, or the realisation that there could be something more from two friends as they quietly sit and talk.

The main focus though is your description of the first physical contact. How does your character feel as they, or the person opposite, move forward and begin the kiss? Describe the physical sensations that pass through your body, and the feelings and thoughts that run through your mind. Does the action bring back happy, or sad, memories of previous kisses? Is this the first kiss ever? What hopes of the future does this kiss bring?

If you are using these prompts for fantasy ideas, then who is it you are kissing? Is the kiss shared with the same 'species'? If your character is alone, perhaps in space, then the kiss will be a remembered one. What if your spacefaring character is with others on the spaceship? Will a kiss cause problems for the other crew members?

Enjoy this prompt, and enjoy your kiss. Feel free to take the kiss further if you want. One kiss may lead to another, and another, and then... well you get the idea, but don't say it was me that led you astray!

"It could be nothing, but I thought I saw something, a moment in her eyes that could mean everything ..."

NOTES

Draw on your memories, the emotions, the sensations that you have and write. There is no minimum or maximum word count, just write and see where your creativity leads you.

At the bar 23

Today's prompt is once again about exploring the art of conversation. However, art may be too strong a word. We're going to delve into the conversation as it mixes with alcohol. Those times when the things we shouldn't say are sometimes said.

The setting is up to you, but the most obvious would be to place yourself at a bar. For this prompt you'll need another person to talk to, but, unless you really want to explore the setting, that is all you need. The conversation is down to you as well. It could be a discussion about your relationship, something that happened in the past or the latest political or sporting scandal.

Once you have your setting and discussion idea, let the conversation flow... and the alcohol! Your characters need to be on the wrong side of sober. They don't need to be drunk, but they do need to be at the stage where their inhibitions have dropped. You'll need to dig deep into your memories if you no longer drink. Or use your imagination if you're not yet of that age, or have never drunk alcohol. If you want, feel free to have just one of the characters drinking. The idea will work fine with just one party drinking, or perhaps you are one sober mind in crowd of inebriation - this can be quite frightening as you see inhibitions dropped.

Try to bring out the false confidence that alcohol brings. The discussion at many a bar could solve all of the world's problems if you listen closely. Unfortunately that false hope disappears in the new dawn, replaced by that headache and regret.

Fantasy and sci-fi writers can create their own brand of alcohol, but again explore how conversation is different when inhibitions drop. If you're on a spaceship, what are the rules for alcohol? Have you been making your own in the science lab? Have fun, but don't drink too much!

" 'And another thing, they think they can just walk in there and expect no response' ... "

NOTES

Draw on your memories, the emotions, the sensations that you have and write. There is no minimum or maximum word count, just write and see where your creativity leads you.

24 Gogglebox

What's your relationship with the TV. Is it the demon that sucks away your time in the corner of the room? Is it a friend you snuggle up to and spend the late nights with? Do you even have a TV? Well, the TV is the centre of our writing prompt today, but there is no time to watch it, it's time to write.

At some point in your day, most likely the evening, you find yourself in front of your TV, or a TV. The choice of program, is up to you. It could be a favourite drama, something you remember watching as a child, or the latest news broadcast. You may be browsing the channels, skipping from one to another, looking for something of interest. You can be watching with a friend, or on your own, the setting is down to you.

What is the program you are watching, or have caught yourself watching? How does it make you feel? Does it bring back memories? Does it shock you in a good way, making you want to see more? Do you remember how you felt the first time you ever watched your favourite program - if you have one? If it is the news, what events are you being misinformed about? If you despise TV then you can use the prompt to remember why you no longer watch it. However, writing about something that we don't do, or even agree with, is a good skill to develop.

For those writing from a fantasy point of view, this could be a little more difficult. You could use a band of travelling performers, or minstrels. Instead of watching the TV you could watch them? In space, TV may have advanced, it could be full-immersion holographic entertainment. However, the prompt is still the same, we are exploring how an external stimulus makes us feel.

"It was the theme tune that triggered the memories ..."

NOTES

Draw on your memories, the emotions, the sensations that you have and write. There is no minimum or maximum word count, just write and see where your creativity leads you.

25   Pastime

This writing prompt is all about doing hobbies. It is all about describing the pastimes that we enjoy and spend our time doing.

The hobby is down to you, as is the location. It could be something as simple as reading or active as skydiving - although why you would enjoy skydiving is beyond me, I feel nauseous a few rungs up a ladder. As you write you should describe how you do your hobby and why. What is the process, what do you need to do and how do you do it? Describing something you do regularly is harder than you think. The steps you take become obvious the more we do them, so to write them down as a full description needs you to focus.

Why you do something is to tap into the emotions that surround your hobby. What do you get out of it? Where is the pleasure and the joy? If your hobby is creative, at what stage do you get most joy, the beginning, the middle, or the end?

Fantasy writers, is your hobby something that those beyond your world will know? Do you need to describe it with invented words? The same questions apply for why, but the how may be quite a challenge.

It is good to have a hobby, a pastime. What if that hobby is writing? You could tie yourself up in a creative writing loop as you do this prompt, as your character does this prompt, as their character does this prompt, as... (At this point you may have turned into Stephen King, but then that is no bad thing - with certain caveats.)

"It was the escapism that was really behind it all ..." **NOTES**

Draw on your memories, the emotions, the sensations that you have and write. There is no minimum or maximum word count, just write and see where your creativity leads you.

Time to relax   26

It is time to relax, to unwind and to let everything melt away, in our words at least. Today's writing prompt is about exploring the moment when you let everything go and chill out. It is a journey into our own minds.

First set the scene, the most obvious is to run a nice hot bath. Depending on how you do this, the ritual of lighting candles, and choosing the right oils, scents and other additives, becomes part of the relaxing progress. However, it doesn't have to be a bath, but it must be somewhere that you, your character can relax.

As you write explore the moment when your relaxation begins. Like the creativity exercise, the moment you relax can begin with just the thought of a bath, or your chosen moment. Do you feel guilty for taking time out for yourself? Are there issues that should have been dealt with? How do you let them go? Are you satisfied with the day so far and therefore feel no regrets about this moment of indulgence?

Write through this time, step by step and emotional thought by emotional thought. Do you drift off to sleep? How do you feel when you let that issue go? This prompt works easy in a fantasy setting. Just choose the situation where you can relax and then explore the process and feelings.

Don't relax too much though imagining what you'll write. As with all these prompts, and with being a writer in general, the first rule is to actually write. Think about the situation, the setting, the feelings, and off you go - write.

"I turned the iPhone off, it seemed like I had disconnected from civilisation, which was just what was required ..."

NOTES

Draw on your memories, the emotions, the sensations that you have and write. There is no minimum or maximum word count, just write and see where your creativity leads you.

27 Street drama

As we write it is easy to think that all the drama happens to us. Our main characters are the ones that move the story, but things happen to others as well. This writing prompt explores things that go bump in the night, to others.

The scene is simple. You are safe and sound, in your own home or apartment. Then you hear a noise. What is it? You look out your window, or open your door and you see...? That's it, what do you see? The choice is yours, describe what is happening.

Something is happening on the street or in your building, concerning your neighbours or people passing by. There might have been an accident, or a dispute? Has an ambulance been called? Have the police arrived? Who is involved and how are they acting? This will give you the chance to describe characters and their actions in depth.

What is happening is down to you, as is the resolution, but the main focus is on describing the event and the people involved. If you are writing fantasy you may need to elaborate on exactly where you are. If you are sleeping out at night, as you journey, how do you see the events happening? Do you hear a noise and then peer through a bush to see what is taking place? Are you woken as you sleep in an inn? A space setting may be more difficult, but if you are on a spaceship with others, it can be easily adapted. If you are on your own, you'll be describing something outside your ship, a meteor shower, space debris, aliens?

Drama, in our writing, doesn't always involve us. Enjoy writing about others in today's prompt. Observing events and retelling them is an essential in storytelling.

> "Thunder reverberates, it is multilayered. The crack I heard was finite, short and sharp ..."

NOTES

Draw on your memories, the emotions, the sensations that you have and write. There is no minimum or maximum word count, just write and see where your creativity leads you.

The blackout

28

You are relaxed at home, the day is coming to a close. You might be watching the TV or reading a book, as always the choice is yours. You might be with a partner, a friend or two, the whole family, or you might be alone. All of a sudden the lights go out and you find yourself in total darkness.

There has been a power cut, but you don't know that yet. Today's prompt is about how you feel and what you do when the lights go out. What is the first thing you do? How do you feel? Are you afraid of the dark? Afraid for yourself or for others, your family, children perhaps? Do you have a set routine for when this happens? Do you know where the torch or candles are? How long is it till you remember there is a flashlight on your phone? How long does the battery in your phone or torch last?

Is the power cut local, just your house or the whole street? Can you see further afield? If you are several floors up in an apartment, how far can you see? How widespread is the blackout? As it draws out do you feel less or more apprehensive about things? Do you find neighbours and discuss what is going on?

If you are on a spaceship, then a power cut is a very serious thing. What emotions run through your head in space? Are you more or less in control of your feelings as your training kicks in? If you are writing in a fantasy setting you'll need to adapt things slightly, perhaps all the candles have gone out, or the flames from the fire and torches have been extinguished? What could have plunged your world into darkness?

The lights have gone out, which means it is time to write. Light a candle stub and find your quill. Explore your feelings and emotions as you come face to face with the dark.

"In one moment we went from an advanced civilisation to something that resembled our stone-age ancestors ..."

NOTES

Draw on your memories, the emotions, the sensations that you have and write. There is no minimum or maximum word count, just write and see where your creativity leads you.

29 Shutdown

The day is coming to an end, and that's where our writing prompt takes us. Everything that has been done during the day has been done, there is nothing else you can do. Some things will need to be left for tomorrow, and they can all wait. This is all about the process of shutting down.

As you prepare for bed and, hopefully, a good night's rest, what do you do? Are there things to clean up, dishes, clothes, toys? What equipment needs to be shutdown and turned off? Do you leave the computer and phone on? Why? Are there pets that need that final moment of care, or walk, or bit of food? Do you need to check on the children?

What things do you do for yourself as you prepare for sleep? Is there time for a shower, a wash, or just the very basics? Do you aim to go straight to sleep or will there be a late night book read, TV watch or Facebook browse? Is there a moment of spiritual, or meditative, reflection? Depending on how, and what, you are writing, is there a partner to whom you need to say something, an apology, an encouragement?

If you are a fantasy writer on a quest, how do you secure your campsite for the night? What do you need to do to ensure you get rest through the dark hours? On a spaceship, the shutdown sequence may be more complicated, or it may be simpler if there are automatic systems, or you have an advanced computer, but there will be a process.

It may surprise you how much you do in order to do nothing, apart from sleep. This prompt is for you to explore that process, to think through the little things that seem innocuous, but which play an important and regular part in the lives of our characters.

"I pinched the ridge of my nose and squeezed my eyes shut for a moment, tiredness has crept up ..."

NOTES

Draw on your memories, the emotions, the sensations that you have and write. There is no minimum or maximum word count, just write and see where your creativity leads you.

30 Sleep, perchance to dream

That's it, the day is over, it is time to sleep. This is where our final writing prompt leads us. It brings us to the moment when we settle down and drift from consciousness to unconsciousness. It is time to sleep, and perhaps we shall dream.

You've had a long day, everything that has happened has been and now it is time to rest. Set the scene describing your final moments before you get into bed, or wherever you are going to sleep. What are the final things you do before turning off the light? How does it feel as you 'lay me down to sleep'? Do you have a comfortable bed, futon, sleeping bag? Are you indoors or out? What are the sounds you can hear? Are the stars shining overhead or do the street lamps glow beyond your windows?

As you begin to drift off, what thoughts are going through your mind? Are you happy with the events of the day? Are there things you'll need to address tomorrow? Were there missed opportunities? Are you glad it is over so you can begin again tomorrow? Do you offer up a little prayer? A prayer of thanks? Or an angry one?

As you fall asleep, do you begin to dream? As you drift into the night and your mind dreams, are there thoughts that take on new meaning, new understanding, new desires? What happens when you are asleep? Feel free to write your dream, this is all about writing what you want, and however much you want. Fantasy writers don't need to change anything to this prompt, everyone sleeps, or at least tries. Unless you are writing about a new form of sentient life, and if you are, then it's up to your imagination to weave in a sleep scene... are they watching someone else?

"My mattress welcomed me like a long lost relative, it's embrace all-encompassing ..." **NOTES**

Draw on your memories, the emotions, the sensations that you have and write. There is no minimum or maximum word count, just write and see where your creativity leads you.

You've reached the end of A Day in the Life. I hope you have found it helpful and begun to enjoy a long-term writing habit. You could always start over again! The wonderful thing about this writing process is that you can reuse it. A Day in the Life is valid for any character you write.

You'll find plenty more hints and tips on writing (and other creative endeavours) at Imaginality (www.yourimaginality.com) where I enable each and every one of us to reach our creative potential.

If you'd like to take your writing further sign up for *A Ticket To Write* (www.tickettowrite.com) an e-course, using video, PDFs and a forum, that leads you through the basics of crafting a believable narrative. In this course we look at characters, locations (worlds), scenes, plots and how to pull it all together into your very own novel. There are prompts and exercises to develop your writing skills and craft. I may even be persuaded to offer a little coaching, though there are limited opportunities for this due to time constraints.

Whatever you decide, have fun and continue writing!

A Day in the Life
How to create your character quickly:

1 The moment you wake
2 Mirror, mirror
3 Breakfast at the author's
4 Open sesame
5 The journey is the destination
6 Arrive and shine
7 The daily plan it
8 Ring, ring
9 Time for tea
10 Back to work, back to reality
11 Let's do lunch
12 It's siesta tone
13 Something, but what?
14 Shocking the system
15 Comfortably calm
16 School run
17 What's the song?
18 Daydream believer
19 A night out
20 The dinner party
21 Play away
22 Just one kiss
23 At the bar
24 Gogglebox
25 Pastime
26 Time to relax
27 Street drama
28 The blackout
29 Shutdown
30 Sleep, perchance to dream

Use this character sheet to note down important facts about your character.

Name:

Age: **Race:** **Sex:**

Physical characteristics:

Height:

Eyes:

Spouse / partner: **Hair:**

Parents:

Children:

Favourite phrase:

Historical era:

Dislikes:

Likes:

Notes:

Defining moment in their past:

A downloadable (and probably updated) version is available at
www.yourimaginality.com/a-day-in-the-life/

Printed in Poland
by Amazon Fulfillment
Poland Sp. z o.o., Wrocław